my first book of **yoga**

Miranda Morgan

GEORGETOWN
PUBLICATIONS

GEORGETOWN
PUBLICATIONS

This edition first published in Canada in 2003 by Georgetown Publications Inc.

1 3 5 7 9 10 8 6 4 2

Georgetown Publications Inc.
579 Richmond Street West, Suite 100
Toronto, Ontario M5V 1Y6
Canada

A CIP catalog record for this book is available from the National Library of Canada

ISBN 0-9731994-2-3

Conceived and produced by Elwin Street Limited
35 Charlotte Road
London EC2A 3PD

Designer: Adelle Morris
Photographer: Mike Prior
Model: Lucy Baldwin

Printed in Singapore

contents

what is **yoga?**

what is **yoga?**

Yoga is the oldest physical discipline in existence, dating back more than 5,000 years. The word "yoga" comes from the Sanskrit word *yuj*, which means "union." By taking care of themself, it is believed that a student of yoga (a yogi) will connect with the Supreme Universal Spirit (Paramatma) that runs through everything.

So what does all that mean?

Well for a start, don't let the weird words worry you. Yoga is a toolbox for well-being, a science rather than a religion, and the words are just a reflection of yoga's ancient tradition. Yoga is also not just very old but incredibly popular, reckoned to be the most widely practiced health system in the world today.

The reason for this is simple; yoga works. Yoga reduces stress, gives you a more flexible body, and relaxes the mind, leaving you feeling healthy, confident, and content. It has helped people lose weight, stop smoking, and develop better concentration. A workout can be easy, intense, or somewhere in between, and different styles allow you to find a practice that suits your individual needs. Best of all, yoga is for everyone, regardless of gender, age, size, income, or beliefs.

It's worth remembering that yoga is very, very old. The timeline opposite highlights a few of the important dates from ancient India to the present day. ▶

B.C. 3000 Earliest references to yoga developed and refined by Vedic people of northern India.

B.C. 500 Upanishads written, including Bhagavad-Gita, a classic of Indian literature, which contains much yogic philosophy.

A.D. 200 Patanjali, "the father of modern yoga", writes the Yoga Sutras, in which he describes the path of raja yoga ("royal" or "classical" yoga) that systemizes yoga into an "eightfold path."

1300s Yoga masters write the Hatha-Yoga-Pradipika, a physical-spiritual guide that defines hatha yoga, the physical yoga style that most people use today.

1800s & early 1900s Yoga masters travel more widely and the West begins to learn about yoga.

1947 Indra Devi opens her yoga studio in Hollywood.

1960s The Beatles travel to India and everything Eastern becomes popular with the hippy movement.

1990s People become bored with the pump and sweat of modern gyms and begin to opt for more holistic exercise forms like yoga, which sees a massive increase in popularity.

Present day Yoga is now practiced by millions of people worldwide. Celebrity yogis include Jane Fonda, Woody Harrelson, Madonna, Sting, and Evander Holyfield.

the **benefits**

Toned body Yoga helps to improve overall body shape and trim excess body fat.

Flexibility Yoga keeps the body flexible so muscles work properly and energy flows freely.

Strength Yoga helps to strengthen the spine and the deep muscles that support us and hold our bodies together.

Pain relief Yoga can improve the workings of the internal organs and endocrine system and ease conditions like back pain and arthritis.

Anti-ageing Yoga slows down the ageing process.

Rejuvenation Yoga creates energy and decreases tension.

Good posture Yoga lengthens the spine, improves posture, and helps you walk tall.

Relaxation Yoga is a real stress buster, countering the rush of modern life. It can give you an oasis of calm in an otherwise hectic day.

Improved concentration Yoga improves your concentration, making you more focused and alert in the rest of your life.

Control over emotions Yoga gives you control over your emotions, including anger and anxiety.

Well-being Yoga releases endorphins and promotes a happy, positive attitude. If you're doing it right, yoga will put a smile on your face.

the **branches**

About 85 percent of people who practice yoga practice Hatha yoga, the physical discipline, but there are other branches in the yoga tradition, each one offering a different path to the ultimate goal: enlightenment.

Hatha yoga

The path of physical discipline. Hatha yoga is the physical form of yoga that most of us would recognize. Hatha yoga emphasizes postures (asanas), breathing techniques (pranayama), and meditation (dhyana) to create a better sense of well-being. About half of the 200 asanas are practiced in the West and they range from lying down flat to tying yourself in improbable knots. Asanas focus the mind and are a great way of coming back to the self.

Central to hatha yoga is the notion of balance. “Ha” means the sun and “tha” means the moon. Hatha yoga is therefore the union between opposites, and healthy balance is seen as the bedrock of a happy life. Yoga is a work-in as well as a work-out.

Raja yoga

The path of meditation. Referred to as “royal” or “classical” yoga, this is a meditative path that attempts to gain enlightenment through the mastery of thought. Raja is the yoga form laid out in Patanjali’s Yoga Sutra, complete with the eightfold path.

Bhakti yoga

The path of devotion. Bhakti yoga is yoga of the heart, a positive way to channel the emotions by seeing the divine in everything. It helps us to cultivate acceptance and tolerance for everyone we meet.

Jnana yoga

The path of knowledge or wisdom. Jnana yoga is the path of the sage or scholar that requires the development of the intellect through study.

Karma yoga

The path of service. What we experience today is created by our past actions. Karma yoga emphasises selfless action so that we can create a better future for everyone.

Mantra yoga

The path of action through sound. There are many different mantras in yoga, all of which help harmonize the system, but the best-known and most potent sound is OM (pronounced "aummm"). This is the symbol of the absolute reality, the Self or spirit. Give it a go. You might enjoy it.

Tantra yoga

The path of continuity and energy release. Tantra yoga isn't all about sex. Tantra yoga is about ritual and experiencing the Divine in everything we do (which just happens to include sex as well).

the **eightfold path**

Patanjali laid out an eightfold path as a series of "limbs" in his Yoga Sutras in A.D. 200, which remain the basic guidelines on how to live a purposeful life with yoga. Even if you don't get as far as number eight (we're talking enlightenment, here, after all) then each stage still contains worthwhile wisdom.

1 Yamas: the "don'ts" of yoga

Yoga has an ethical basis in social behavior. The first stage is to do the right thing in society. The yamas aim to purify the mind. They are the "don't do" things in yoga, and can be found in all the world's major religions.

Don't be violent Be kind in your actions, words, or thoughts, to yourself and those around you.

Don't lie Truth does no harm. It's not always easy to uncover, but it makes us stronger in the end.

Don't steal We must resist the desire for what doesn't belong to us or risk living in a state of unfulfilled wanting. Learn to enjoy the simple things in life.

Don't have sex without love Learn the art of self-control. Respect your partner and hold back from meaningless sexual encounters.

Don't be greedy Try to live simply. There's a big difference in life between want and need.

2 Niyamas: the "dos" of yoga

The second stage on the eightfold path deals with your attitudes toward yourself, which means taking responsibility for your own actions. Niyamas are therefore the positive observances or "dos" of yoga. In the Yoga Sutra, Patanjali lists five:

Be pure This is a cleanliness of your physical body and surroundings so wash and wear clean clothes. But it is also a purity of mind and living, so practice the five yamas and try to live an uncluttered, simple life.

Be content Be happy with who you are and what you have. Try to look at things in a positive light. Continue to cultivate inner growth, but have patience and trust that if things are bad they will improve.

Show self-control Self-control is not about denying yourself things but looking after yourself. It's also about maintaining an enthusiasm for whatever you are doing and sticking with it until the end; that way you'll see results.

Study This means studying not just texts or scriptures but yourself as well. Look at yourself closely but kindly, perhaps keeping a journal, and you'll see everything else more clearly.

Show devotion If you turn all your energy and love to what is good in you and the world then positive energy will flow back into everything that you do.

3 Asanas: the postures

The postures have evolved throughout the centuries to give a complete workout to the whole body, inside and out. They ease tense muscles, tone up the internal organs, and improve the flexibility of the body's joints and ligaments. Don't forget that yoga is intelligent exercise; each posture should be a combination of mind, body, and breath within that moment. Asana means steady pose, and Patanjali describes steadiness and the ability to remain comfortable as key to any posture. Take things easy, stage by careful stage. Postures should be carried out in slow, fluid movements and combined to form graceful routines. Many teachers will use the Sanskrit names for the poses, so it is useful to familiarize yourself with them. Modern yoga has about 200 postures, but you can develop a perfectly good program with about 30.

4 Pranayama: breath control

Most of us take breathing for granted, using perhaps one third of our lung capacity, but we would be helpless without it. Breathing both refreshes and rejuvenates, and is intimately connected with the mind and the emotions. In yoga, entire books have been written about the breath. Breath is the life force (prana) and a yogin (master of yoga) will measure his life not in years but in the number of breaths taken in his lifetime. You can practice pranayama as an isolated technique or as a part of your daily routine.

5 Pratyahara: withdrawal of the senses

Pratyahara encourages us to direct our attention inward and draw our awareness away from the external world. This inner focus can happen during breathing exercises, meditation, yoga postures, or any activity requiring concentration. The reason for cutting ourselves off in this way is to stop our senses controlling us and, if you wish to go further along the eightfold path, to continue the search for an ultimate truth by turning inward. Watch less TV and switch off the radio. Practice deep relaxation and meditation. If you're not quite up to that, then detachment is a great technique for pain control and an excellent way to deal with uncomfortable symptoms or chronic conditions.

6 Dharana: concentration

Modern life can all be a bit much, a place where "multi-tasking" is seen as a virtue and it can often be difficult to concentrate on any one thing at a time. So why not learn to focus on one thing at a time and get the most out of it? Dharana encourages you to let go of all the stuff and nonsense flying around inside your head except that which you are concentrating on. In yogic practice, that point of focus might be a flower, a flame, a mantra, or a specific part of the body. By clearing the mind, Dharana prepares the mind for meditation, the seventh limb. Mental exercises, like many physical exercises, can seem daunting at first, but you and your mind will improve over time.

7 Dhyana: meditation

An ancient healer once stated "Man is ill, because he is never still," and meditation is about finding a point of stillness between the end of one thought and the beginning of another. In meditation we practice being the observer rather than the doer; remaining neutral toward our thoughts means we do not lend them energy to disturb our mind. Many people think of it as an emptying out or nothingness, but in fact it is a heightened state of awareness, a state when you feel more awake and alive than before. Meditation can reduce blood pressure, relieve stress, aid healing, and increase your intelligence. It's a difficult task, but not impossible, and well worth the effort. And it's also only one step away from enlightenment.

8 Samadhi: enlightenment

All paths lead to enlightenment, the ultimate goal of goals. It can seem a bit of a tall order, since enlightenment is a permanent feeling of ecstatic fulfillment in which you transcend the self and become one with the Supreme Universal Spirit (Paramatma). But if all that sounds a bit much, then enlightenment can also be looked upon as the fulfilment of your potential, as being more alive to the best of yourself. You may not reach it in this life time, but you can still reach toward it, since enlightenment brings what we most aspire to in our lives: joy, fulfillment, and peace.

you and **yoga**

you and **yoga**

People come to yoga for many different reasons. Each person will have a different goal, whether that means wanting to relax, touch their toes, correct their posture, or connect with something more spiritual in their lives. It is worth thinking about what you want because it will determine where and how you take your practice of yoga further.

Are you simply curious?
There's only one way to satisfy your curiosity. Go along to a yoga class and try it out.

Are you looking for a fitness program?
Yoga provides a full workout, so don't be surprised if you start feeling good about yourself, inside and out. Just go easy on yourself. After all, Madonna wasn't built in a day.

Are you into sports?
Yoga can be a great supplement to most sports, from football to swimming, improving strength, balance, and control. In Latin America yoga is becoming popular as an exhibition sport, but yoga at its heart is non-competitive.

Are you looking for help with a physical or mental illness?
Yoga can improve the workings of your body and mind and help alleviate pain. However, therapy should be pursued with an experienced teacher. Always consult a physician before taking up a new form of exercise and always tell your yoga teacher if you have any specific health concerns.

Are you pregnant?
Congratulations! Yoga has numerous benefits to help you through pregnancy. Consult a doctor first and look for special prenatal classes in your area.

Are you looking for a change of lifestyle?
Some people live, breath, eat, and sleep yoga. If you do enjoy it then apply the wisdom of yoga to your everyday life.

Do you feel a spiritual lack?
Some people are looking to add or deepen a spiritual dimension in their lives. Yoga can foster and promote this, and lead you on a path of self discovery with the ultimate goal of enlightenment.

What are you like?
Do you jump with joy at the thought of physical exercise or do you start whining if you have to walk farther than your car? Do you worry most about your body or are you far too busy cultivating your intellect? Do you look on the bright side of life, or do you live under a black cloud? Develop your yoga practice with honesty, curiosity, and enthusiasm.

Remember, you're the one who's going to be breathing and moving and thinking out there on the mat. Take responsibility for your own practice and you'll enjoy it a hundred times more.
What follows is a guide to the major yoga styles. It's important to find one that suits you, so as you read through them, think about what you are looking for and what you are like.

yoga **styles**

Hatha yoga is the generic term for the physical branch that forms the basis of most yoga classes. In its long history, and especially since its introduction to the West, Hatha yoga has developed into many different styles, including some that offer a more physical and energetic approach (like Ashtanga) and others that are more meditative (like Ananda). Each is a matter of personal preference, so it is worthwhile finding out which yoga suits you.

Kundalini: awakening energy

What's different Kundalini is a powerful yoga used to wake a reservoir of energy known as the serpent power (literally translated as "she who is coiled") stored at the base of the spine. Once released, this cosmic power travels up the spine to the crown of the head. It brings about this energy shift through asanas and breath control, with particular emphasis on chanting and meditation. Kundalini yoga can be very powerful and should always be taught by an experienced teacher.

History Once a closely guarded secret in India, Kundalini yoga arrived in the United States in 1969, when Sikh master Yogi Bhajan challenged tradition and began to teach it publicly. There are now more than 1,500 Kundalini teachers worldwide. Yogi Bhajan is also the founder and spiritual head of Healthy, Happy, Holy Organization (3HO) with headquarters in Los Angeles and branches throughout the world.

Ashtanga: fast-paced yoga

What's different A very physical workout calling for strength, flexibility, and stamina, Ashtanga is taught in a series of fast-paced sequences beginning with sun salutations. Ashtanga aims to strengthen and purify the nervous system, allowing energy to flow up through the spine.

History Originated with K. Pattabhi Jois, a principal disciple of Shri Krishnamacharya, a teacher of many yoga masters. The Ashtanga Yoga Institute is in Mysore, India. Ashtanga yoga is increasingly popular, especially since celebrity endorsement by Madonna and Sting. Power yoga, made popular by Beryl Bender Birch, is based on Ashtanga.

Bikram: hot yoga

What's different This is a hot, vigorous, sweaty workout since the room temperature is raised to between 85 and 100 degrees Fahrenheit during a class. Students perform 26 poses, always in the same order, designed to cleanse the body from the inside out. Needless to say, you have to be quite fit to give hot yoga a go.

History Based on the teaching of Bikram Choudhury, who achieved fame as yoga teacher to the Hollywood stars. He now teaches at centers around the world including Bombay, San Francisco, and Tokyo. His teachings have been adapted by other teachers.

Integral: the healing power

What's different Integral yoga is a gentle style that aims to integrate different yoga styles with a combination of postures. The classes follow a set format and place great importance on breath control and meditation. Form takes second place to function, which means that it should be quite a comfortable class to take.

History Swami Satchidananda taught the crowds at Woodstock in 1969 to chant "om" for peace. There are now more than forty branches worldwide of his Integral Yoga Institute. His student, Dr. Dean Ornish, uses integral yoga as part of his treatment of heart patients.

Kripalu: yoga of consciousness

What's different Kripalu is a more meditative, internally focused yoga taught in three stages, one-to-one. Stage one calls for the steady practice of postures, held for a short duration only. Stage two entails holding the postures for longer periods and becoming more meditative. In stage three the practice of posture becomes a "meditation-in-motion," in which yogis can do postures spontaneously.

History Developed by Yogi Amrit Desai and now taught around the world. Every year, 12,000 yogis congregate at the 300-acre Kripalu Center in Lenox, Massachussetts, for the "Kripalu experience."

Iyengar: symmetry and alignment

What's different Probably the most widely practiced style of Hatha yoga, Iyengar is a vigorous yoga characterised by precision performance; a great deal of attention is paid to the details of the postures as students progress from beginners to advanced. Each pose is held for longer than in most other yoga styles. Iyengar yoga also uses various props, including cushions, benches, and straps.

History Created by B.K.S. Iyengar. There are thousands of well-qualified, well-trained Iyengar teachers worldwide and B.K.S. Iyengar's book, *Ray of Light*, remains an indispensable guide to yoga.

Viniyoga: gentle flow

What's different Considered excellent for beginners and increasingly used in therapeutic environments, Viniyoga places great emphasis on coordinating the breath with sequential process (called vinyasa-krama). Viniyoga also incorporates sound, ritual and meditation. Postures are done with slightly bended knees and attention is focused on the spine. Teaching is usually one-to-one.

History Developed by Shri Krishnamacharya, who taught B.K.S. Iyengar, Pattabhi Jois, and Indra Devi. Viniyoga has since been carried on by his son T.K.V. Desikachar, whose school is in Madras, India.

Ananda: emphasis on meditation

What's different A gentle style designed to prepare the student for meditation. Ananda yoga uses affirmations while in asanas as the student moves from body awareness through energy awareness to, finally, silent awareness. Ananda also includes unique energization exercises, first developed in 1917, which involve directing the body's energy or life force to different organs and limbs.

History Anchored in the teachings of Paramhansa Yogananda, developed by an American pupil known as Swami Kriyananda. The Ananda World Brotherhood Village is situated in Nevada City, California.

Sivananda: healthy lifestyle

What's different Relaxed and gentle, Sivananda yoga combines all the branches of yoga: asanas, pranayama, self-less service, prayer, chanting, meditation, and self-study. It offers a gentle approach that takes the student through the twelve sun salutation postures and incorporates chanting, meditation, and deep relaxation in each session. Students are also encouraged to embrace a healthy lifestyle.

History Swami Sivananda founded Sivananda yoga. His disciple, Swami Vishnu-devananda, founded the Sivananda Yoga Vedanta Centre in Montreal in 1959 and published *The Complete Illustrated Book of Yoga*.

before you **begin**

Practice yoga on an empty stomach That means at least four hours after a heavy meal or two hours after a snack. Drink water before the practice.

Wear comfortable clothes Make sure your clothes are loose-fitting and have bare feet.

Find a quiet place Practice in a quiet area or an empty room, on a folded mat or carpeted floor. The atmosphere should be relaxed, without music or conversation.

Yoga is not a race If you are in a class, don't worry about what the person next to you is doing; yoga is meant to be non-competitive.

Find a good teacher You can learn yoga with books, videos, DVDs, tapes, or CDs, but nothing beats learning yoga face-to-face. A good teacher will be able to establish a correct routine and a regular class will give you a solid basis to motivate you in your practice. Have a look around your local area and see what's on offer, talk to the teacher and get a feel for the class. A good teacher will have studied yoga thoroughly, will know about physiology, will be able to adapt techniques for the individual, and will not confuse religious or personal beliefs with yoga.

Be realistic Try and integrate yoga into your life; anything between one and six times a week is good. Try and practice regularly, but don't punish yourself if you take a break; be kind and return to it happily.

Take care As with all exercise routines, you should seek medical advice first, especially if you already suffer from an illness or injury. Read the "Take Care" sections throughout the book and refrain from doing anything that causes pain. Don't practice asanas or pranayama if you have a fever and take things easy during menstruation.

Be sensible There's no point jumping into Ashtanga yoga if you're a frail 70 year-old.

Listen to your body It's the only one you've got. Enjoy discovering your body and your mind.

Be patient Bit by gentle bit, yoga will change your life, but mastering yoga takes time…

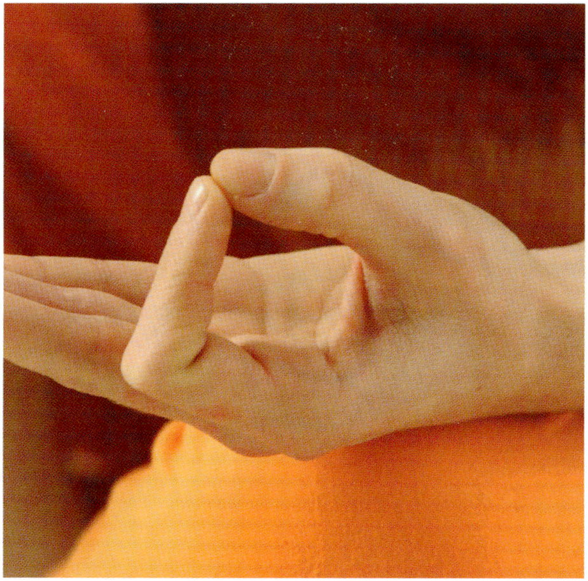

the **asanas**

the **asanas**

Remember balance Asanas refresh the body, mind, and spirit and contribute to well-being. Asanas aim to promote strength and flexibility and at their heart is balance.

Remain comfortable and steady Make sure you practice different asanas to create a balanced sequence. If you do a series of forward stretches, then do backward stretches afterward. If you do an asana that stretches one side of your body, then you always need to repeat the asana on the other side.

Experiment and explore your body It is essential to learn the asana correctly, which is another reason for going to a yoga class. However, the pictures of the yoga postures are the "goal," i.e. the direction you are going toward, not where you need to be. Experiment and explore different positions and alignment to make the posture work for your body.

Three stages Be conscious of the three stages of an asana: getting into the pose, holding the pose, and coming out of the pose.

Breathe throughout Unless otherwise indicated, you should hold asanas for 2-6 breaths. Remember to breathe throughout the asanas.

Follow the guide Take note of the easy-to-use guide below. Make sure you follow the circles to practice the "basic" and "beginners" asanas first.

Above all, enjoy!

● basic ●● beginners ●●● intermediate

the **breath**

Breath control is the foundation of good yoga practice. Dirga Pranayama and Ujjayi Pranayama are two breath techniques that can be used during asanas and practiced throughout the day.

Dirga: the three-part breath

Dirga Pranayama is called the three-part breath because you are actively breathing into three parts of your abdomen. The breath is continuous, inhaled and exhaled through the nose. Inhalation starts in the low belly then moves to the low chest, and finally the low throat. The exhalation reverses the process, starting in the low throat and finishing in the low belly. When you start, you may want to isolate the movement in each position, using the hands. Eventually relax the effort of the Pranayama and breathe into the three positions gently.

Ujjayi: the ocean-sounding breath

Ujjayi Pranayama is called the ocean-sounding breath because you make an ocean sound by contracting the glottis with the inhalation and exhalation. This Pranayama is done through the nose, but you can begin practicing breathing through the mouth. To make the ocean sound, whisper the syllable "hah," feeling the contraction in your throat. After a couple of breaths try to close the mouth, breathing through the nose while still making the ocean sound in your throat.

Sun salutation
(Surya Namaskar)

If you do only one exercise a day, then it should be the sun salutation: a prayer to the sun. The pose involves a sequence of twelve separate, flowing movements. It can be used as a warm-up but you should get it right with a teacher, as it includes a lot of different asanas.

Top tips If you do the sequence first thing in the morning your body might be a little stiff, so take a hot shower or a bath first to warm up your body.

Take care If you suffer from high blood pressure, are pregnant, or have eye problems, have severe arthritis or a bad back, then seek medical advice before starting the sun salutation.

1|12 Body straight; weight even on both feet; head, neck, and shoulders relaxed

2 Inhale; push hips forward; body curves back

9 Inhale; step right leg between hands; front of body open

10 Exhale; fold forward

11 Inhale; hips push forward; body curves back

3 Exhale; fold forward; legs straight; push tail bone up; head in toward knees

4 Inhale; step back right leg; toes on floor; front of body open

5 Retaining the breath, step feet back; straight line from heels to shoulders

6 Exhale, bring shoulders forward of your wrists, hips raised off the floor

7 Inhale; press hands to floor; curve chest up in cobra pose

8 Exhale; tuck toes under and lift hips high; hold for three breaths

Mountain (Tadasana)

The foundation for all of the standing postures, in the mountain pose the entire body must be equally balanced.

Benefits Improves posture and confidence. Balances the body. Focuses the mind.

Top tips Firmly plant your feet into the ground and do not lock knees back. Tilt your hips slightly in, which will tilt your stomach back toward your spine. Good posture is everything, so try and feel the crown of your head pushing toward the ceiling, your spine long and straight.

Take care The weight of your body should be evenly distributed between the toes, balls and heels of your feet.

Triangle
(Trikonasana)

Known as the happy pose, the triangle helps you feel joyful and energetic.

Benefits Engages every part of the body. Tones and stretches leg, hip, and back muscles, as well as the waist. Stimulates bowels and intestines. Improves circulation. Develops the chest.

Top tips Be careful not to bend forward, keeping your hips flat and facing forward.

Take care Stretch only as far as you can.

Warrior I
(Virabhadrasana I)

This pose is both strong and vibrant, as the name suggests.

Benefits Relieves stiffness in the back and shoulders. Strengthens legs. Trims the hips. Tones the abdomen.

Top tips Keep the upper body facing forward as you bend the left leg in.

Take care This pose is strenuous, so avoid it if you have a heart condition or are not very strong. Take extra care if you have arthritic hips.

Standing forward bend
(Pada Hasthasana)

Poses with forward bends soothe the mind and calm the nervous system.

Benefits Lengthens the spinal column. Stretches the entire back of the body. Stimulates digestive, uro-genital, nervous, and endocrine systems.

Top tips From mountain posture. Try and keep the hips facing forward and your back flat. You may have to keep your legs straight and hold on to either calves or ankles.

Take care This pose is strenuous. Avoid if you have a heart condition or are not very strong. Approach with caution if you have lower back pain or sciatica.

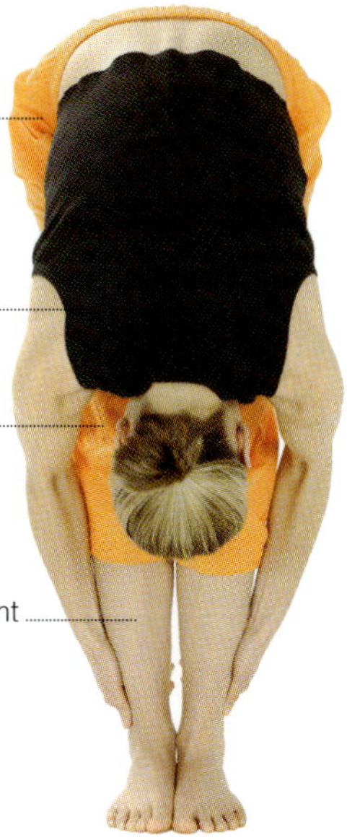

Downward facing dog
(Adho Mukha Shvanasana)

Good for warming up the body and giving your heart a rest.

Benefits Stretches and releases tension in the upper spine and neck. Strengthens and stretches upper body. Stimulates brain and nervous system.

Top tips Lift your pelvis and focus on spine lengthening, not bringing your heels down. Try to distribute your weight evenly between hands and heels.

Take care Do not force your heel to the floor or you will stretch your Achilles tendon. If your back is at all sore then keep your knees bent. Approach with caution if you have arthritic wrists.

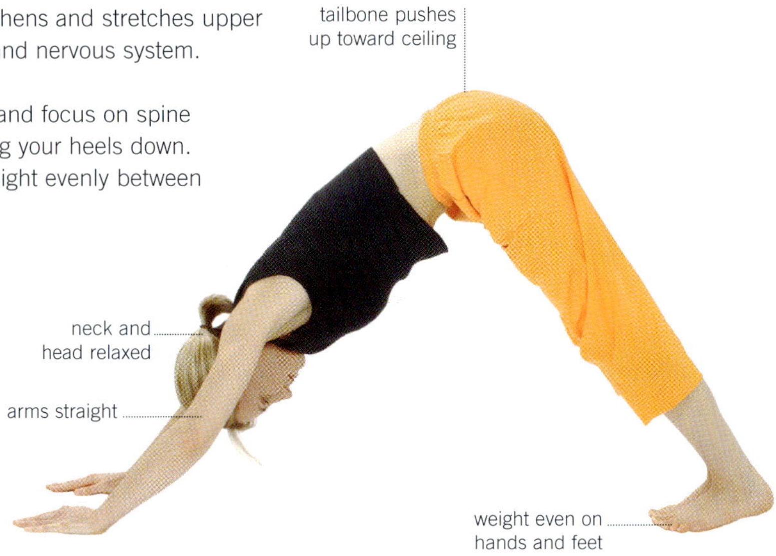

Tree pose (Vrksasana)

Balancing postures improve memory and concentration by engaging your whole mind and body. Keep the eyes focused on a single point throughout.

Benefits Stretches the entire body. Tones leg muscles. Helps balance and concentration.

Top tips Start in mountain pose: 1. Balance on one leg. 2. Draw the other foot to the thigh or calf of the standing leg (never against the knee). 3. Concentrate and raise your hands above your head. Remember to breathe; it will only interfere with your balance if you don't. Keep your hips even by lowering the position of your foot on your inner thigh.

Take care Use a wall as a support behind you if you suffer from vertigo. Do not come out of the posture too quickly.

Easy pose (Sukhasana)

Sukhasana means content or happy. It is the basic pose for sitting and relaxation and a comfortable seated position for meditation.

Benefits Opens the hips. Lengthens the spine. Focuses the mind.

Top tips Try and bring your heels out to sit under the opposite knee and keep your spine straight. Place a folded blanket under knees or under hip bones for extra comfort.

Take care Let your knees drop only as far as comfortable. Take special care if you have a recent or chronic knee or hip injury or inflammation.

Easy pose forward fold
(Sukhasana forward fold)

This is a centering way to start your practice.

Benefits Opens the hips. Lengthens the spine. Focuses the mind.

Top tips Place the fingertips just in front of your legs. Lengthen the side of the torso. When you feel relaxed, slide the hands away.

Take care Always remember to repeat with your legs crossed the other way. Take special care if you have a recent or chronic hip injury or inflammation.

Hero (Virasana)

Benefits Stimulates leg muscles. Opens chest. Helpful for respiratory problems. Calms the whole body.

Top tips As you sit down between your feet, use your fingers to "iron" your calf muscles out to the sides. If the buttocks cannot come on the floor between the feet, place a folded blanket between them. You can also do a very effective forward fold from this pose.

Take care Do not practice if you have knee or hip problems, or varicose veins.

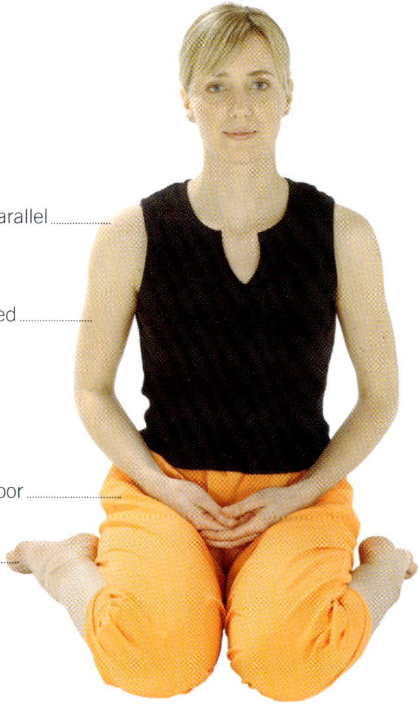

Cobbler's pose
(Baddha Konasana)

This is the position in which shoemakers in India sit to work.

Benefits Aids pelvis, abdomen, and back. Loosens knees and ankles.

Top tips Stretch up: this pose should stretch the spine and inner thighs. If your upper back becomes rounded, leave your feet farther from your body. When your hips loosen and you feel more comfortable in this posture, you will be able to fold forward.

Take care Never force the knees downward. Do not attempt if you have severe knee problems.

Rod or staff (Dandasana)

The rod or staff is the basis for many forward bends.

Benefit Increases your concentration and clarity of focus. The rod is great for body alignment.

Top tips Push your palms lightly down against the ground to create space in your spine. Don't puff out your chest. Imagine your head is being gently pulled upward. Concentrate on your upper body becoming as straight as a rod.

Take care If the pose is uncomfortable, sit on a folded blanket.

Seated forward bend
(Paschimothanasana)

Paschimottanasana is an excellent stretch to the whole of the back of the body.

Benefits Stretches whole back body. Tones the kidneys and abdominal organs. Improves digestion and circulation.

Top tips This may be difficult to begin with, and you might want to loop a rope around your foot to help you hold the pose. If you can, hook your big toes with your index fingers.

Take care Do not bounce in the posture and take extra care if you have back problems or sciatica.

Cat tilt I (Bidalasana I)

A great all-round pose that is good for women during pregnancy.

Benefits Stretches the middle to upper back and shoulders. Alleviates backaches.

Top tips Start with a flat back and exhale to arch upward. Hands, knees, and feet do not move in this posture; only the spine and back move.

Take care Avoid if you have chronic back pain or injury.

Cat tilt II (Bidalasana II)

The cat tilt also reminds us that, in yoga, every posture must be balanced with its opposite.

Benefits Stretches the middle to low back and hips. Lengthens the spine. Stimulates the kidneys and adrenal glands.

Top tips Inhale to arch downward, alternating with the cat tilt. Exhale to finish with a flat back.

Take care Avoid if you have chronic back pain or injury.

Cobra (Bhujangasana)

Backward bends are important for increasing flexibility and opening the organs. They are also great for people who work at computers all day.

Benefits Opens the chest and provides good backward spinal stretch. Tones abdominal organs.

Top tips Use your upper back muscles to arch backward rather than using your hands to push. Keep your elbows in and don't scrunch your shoulders up around your neck.

Take care Stretch your spine slowly, vertebra by vertebra. Take extra care if you have back problems.

Bow (Dhanurasana)

Benefits Improves spinal elasticity. Tones the abdominal organs. Increases vitality.

Top tips Lift your legs and chest off the floor. Done correctly, only your lower abdomen should be touching the floor.

Take care Don't push it too much. Do not practice if you have abdominal problems or high blood pressure, and take extra care if you have knee, hip, or back problems.

Spinal twist/Half Lord of the Fishes
(Ardha Matsyendrasana)

Twisting poses energize the body and increase range of motion and spinal flexibility and are good for relieving stiffness in the neck and shoulder.

Benefits Opens, lengthens, nourishes, and realigns the spine. Improves the nervous system. Aids digestion.

Top tips From the rod pose, bring left leg over right leg and tuck right leg in. Keep your spine erect but do not lift your shoulders. Press down into the left hand, left foot, and right heel to lift and lengthen the spine. Exhale as you revolve the spine to the left. Keep the shoulder blades close into the spine.

Take care Twist only as far as you can. Take extra care if you have abdominal or back problems. As in all asanas, repeat on the other side.

Lying down spinal twist
(Jathara Parivartanasana)

This posture, practiced daily, will quickly strengthen weak abdominal muscles that can cause back pain.

Benefits Tones the spine and strengthens the legs. Also great for easing pain caused by tight back muscles pulling on the vertebrae.

Top tips Lie on your back with your knees bent out close to your chest. Take your arms out to the sides and, keeping your knees bent, slowly drop them to the side. If your knees rise off the floor, use your hand to keep them down.

Take care Remember to roll over and do the other side for balance.

Shoulderstand (Sarvangasana)

The shoulderstand is the queen of the poses, revitalizing the body as it sends fresh blood to the heart and brain. It is usually held for longer than other poses, but should be carried out under the supervision of a trained teacher, especially for the first time.

Benefits The shoulderstand does just about everything. It rejuvenates the entire body, stretches the neck and upper spine. It stimulates the thyroid and parathyroid glands and is a great headache remedy.

Top tips With control, bring your legs and hips in the air and then support your back. Lay your arms out flat on the floor when lifting into the pose. Rest on your shoulders rather than your neck, and roll out of the position slowly. You may want to practice this with a teacher before trying it at home.

Take care The pose is also not for anyone with a neck injury, high blood pressure, or women who are menstruating or pregnant.

Plow (Halasana)

The plow is another excellent pose for all around rejuvenation.

Benefits Stimulates the spine. Strengthens the nervous system. Improves the circulation. Releases neck tension. Relieves constipation. Promotes mental relaxation.

Top tips Keep supporting your back unless your feet touch the floor. Rest on your shoulders rather than your neck, and roll out of the position slowly.

Take care If your toes do not touch the floor, keep supporting your back as in shoulderstand. The pose is not for anyone with a neck injury, or high blood pressure, or women who are menstruating or pregnant.

Fish (Matsyasana)

A good pose for releasing the neck and a counter pose to the shoulderstand and plow. Also a good posture for asthmatics.

Benefits Opens the chest. Helps respiratory problems. Eases neck tension.

Top tips Push the front of the body, opening and expanding the chest. Palms rest on the floor, below buttocks. The weight is on the elbows, not the top of head.

Take care Approach with extreme caution if you have back, neck, or shoulder problems.

Wind-relieving pose
(Apanasana)

Supine postures such as apanasana release stress and promote flexibility.

Benefits Massages abdominal organs and releases gas from the intestines.

Top tips You can also gently rock back and forth in this position to massage the spinal area.

Take care This pose can be strenuous. Do it with caution if you have lower back pain.

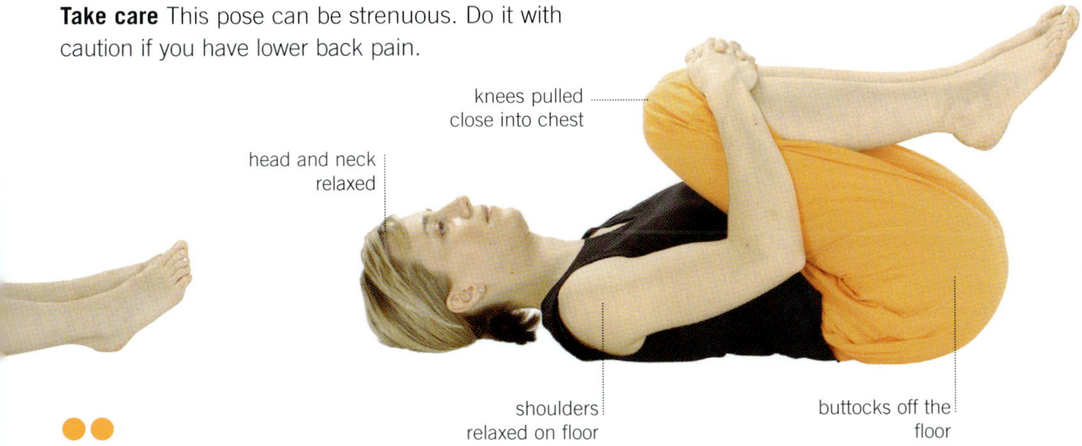

Child's pose (Mudhasana)

Go into this pose whenever you feel tired or need to relax.

Benefits Rejuvenating, relaxing pose. Calms the body, mind, and spirit. Good for relief of lower back and abdominal organs.

Top tips You can vary the pose by stretching your arms in front of you or by your side.

Take care If your knees feel strained, put a pillow or blanket between your knees and your calves.

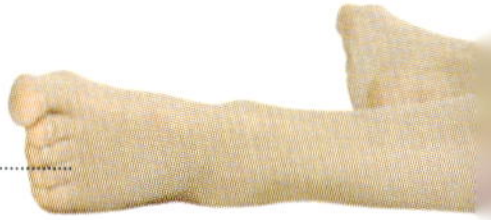

Corpse (Savasana)

A great posture for relieving tension and fatigue at the beginning and end of every yoga session and between asanas. Stay in savasana for 5-15 minutes.

Benefits Relaxes and refreshes the body, mind, and spirit.

Top tips Consciously release and relax any tense areas that you find. If you need to, rock or wiggle that part of your body from side to side. Imagine you are breathing good into your life and breathing out bad.

Take care When you come up, bend the knees to the chest and roll over to one side, coming into a fetal position before pushing yourself up.

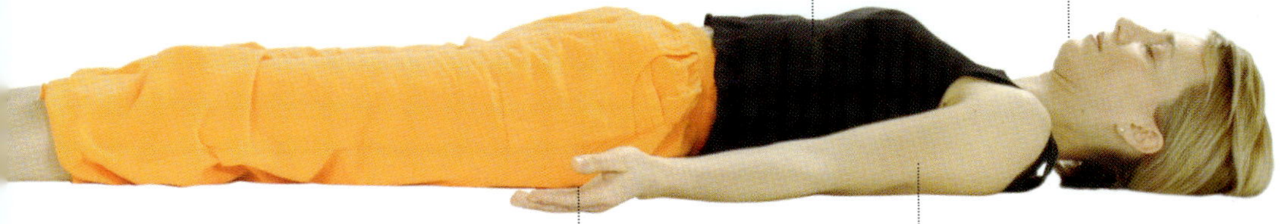

Meditation

Meditation is the focusing of the mind on a single object. As thoughts dissipate, the mind becomes quiet, and we are able to be fully present in the moment. The techniques of meditation might appear simple and easy to learn, but it takes time to focus the mind. The benefits of a regular meditation practice include reduction of stress, anxiety, and frustration, as well as improved memory, concentration, and inner peace.

Beginning meditation: sit in a comfortable position, either cross-legged on the floor or in a chair. Sit with your spine straight, imagining a thread tugging the crown of your head upward. Relax your shoulders and open your chest. Rest your hands on your knees. Relax the face, jaw, tongue, and belly. Lightly close your eyes. Breathe slowly, smoothly, and deeply in and out through the nose, letting the breath rise from your belly to chest. As your breath slows and deepens, let go of any thoughts or distractions. Practice the meditations for 10-20 minutes. To end, gently let the eyes open. Inhale, and with the palms of the hands held together in front of the heart, exhale and gently bow.

Meditation through concentration: allow the mind to focus on the breath. Feel the breath as it moves in and out of the body, moving through the nose, throat, windpipe, and lungs. Feel the body as it rises and falls with each breath. Bring as much of your awareness to your body and breath as possible with each moment. As the thoughts return to the mind, let them go, and return the focus back to the body and breath.

Meditation through mindfulness: alternatively, imagine a clear blue sky, deep and wide. Each time a thought comes into your mind look on it as a drifting cloud. Do not dwell on the cloud, but sit and watch as it passes across the clear sky and leaves as quietly as it has come. Open your eyes, stand up slowly and go into the world with an inner calm.

Wish yourself happy and well, your journey just begun.

glossary

Useful terms

Ananda yoga: A more meditative yoga style.
Anusara yoga: A heart-centered yoga style
Asanas: Postures
Ashtanga yoga: A very physical, athletic yoga style
Bikram yoga: A hot, vigorous, sweaty yoga style done in a sauna-type environment.
Dhyana: Meditation
Eightfold path: The basic guidelines on how to live a purposeful life with yoga.
Hatha yoga: The physical form of yoga that most of us would recognize.
Integral yoga: A gentle yoga style that aims to integrate different styles.
Iyengar yoga: A vigorous yoga style characterized by precision performance.
Kripalu yoga: A meditative yoga style
Kundalini: A powerful yoga style used to awaken energy at the base of the spine.
Niyama: The "do's" of yoga
Paramatma: The Supreme Universal Spirit that runs through everything.
Patanjali: The father of modern yoga, who wrote the Yoga Sutras in A.D. 200.
Power yoga: A vigorous yoga style based on ashtanga.
Pranayama: Breathing techniques.
Samadhi: Enlightenment.
Sivananda yoga: A relaxed and gentle yoga style
Somatic yoga: A gentle, psychophysiological yoga style
Viniyoga: A gentle, recuperative yoga style
Yamas: The "don'ts" of yoga

The asanas

ENGLISH	SANSKRIT
Bow	Dhanurasana
Cat tilt	Bidalasana
Cobbler's pose	Bhaddha Konasana
Child's pose	Mudhasana
Cobra	Bhujangasana
Corpse	Savasana
Downward facing dog	Adho mukha shvanasana
Easy pose	Sukhasana
Fish	Matsyasana
Lying down spinal twist	Jathara Parivatanasana
Mountain	Tadasana

ENGLISH	SANSKRIT
Plow	Halasana
Rod or staff	Dandasana
Seated forward bend	Paschimothanasana
Shoulderstand	Sarvangasana
Spinal twist	Ardha Matsyendrasana
Standing forward bend	Pada Hasthasana
Sun salutation	Surya Namaskar
Tree pose	Vrksasana
Triangle	Trikonasana
Warrior	Virabhadrasana
Wind-relieving pose	Apanasana

further information

For further information and a directory of qualified yoga instructors in your area:
Australia www.iyta.org.au, www.yogaindailylife.org.au
North America www.yogadirectory.com, www.yogafinder.com, www.yogasite.com
General www.yogajournal.com, www.sivananda.org

index